*Did You*

# HULL

## A MISCELLANY

Compiled by Julia Skinner

With particular reference to the work of Graham Wilkinson

# THE FRANCIS FRITH COLLECTION

www.francisfrith.com

Based on a book first published in the United Kingdom in 2006 by The Francis Frith Collection®

This edition published exclusively for Identity Books in 2012 ISBN 978-1-84589-396-5

British Library Cataloguing in Publication Data

Did You Know? Hull - A Miscellany
Compiled by Julia Skinner
With particular reference to the work of Graham Wilkinson

The Francis Frith Collection
Oakley Business Park,
Wylye Road, Dinton,
Wiltshire SP3 5EU
Tel: +44 (0) 1722 716 376
Email: info@francisfrith.co.uk
www.francisfrith.com

Printed and bound in Malaysia

Front Cover: **HULL, CARR LANE 1903** 49816p

*The colour-tinting is for illustrative purposes only, and is not intended to be historically accurate*

# CONTENTS

# INTRODUCTION

Hull, or more correctly Kingston upon Hull, is situated on the north side of the River Humber at a point where the River Hull empties the waters drained from the Holderness Plain of the East Riding of Yorkshire. Kingston upon Hull was granted city status in 1299, although the name and title of the city did not officially become 'The City and County of Kingston upon Hull' until 1977.

Following the construction of Hull's first dock in 1778, then the largest inland dock in the kingdom, trade and the city grew rapidly. So successful was the port that several more docks were to follow during the 19th century, eventually resulting in the city being completely ringed by water. The railway arrived in 1840 with the building of the Hull & Selby Railway. This added to the prosperity of the city, and in turn led to the construction of several more docks to the east and west of Hull to cope with the increase in trade. Hull, the third largest port in Britain, still has docks running for several miles along the north bank of the Humber, handling hundreds of millions of pounds worth of cargo and thousands of passengers every year.

In its day, Hull was the great fishing port of the British Empire, and the port of Hull was once the home of the world's largest deep-water fishing fleet. It is often said that the kipper was invented in Hull! Hull trawlers fished the North Sea, the White Sea, and the fringes of the Arctic, in an industry that was more hazardous than coal mining. Despite savage reductions in the fishing fleet and the EU quota system, Hull remains one of our principal fishing ports, though much of the fish is either landed from foreign trawlers or arrives by lorry from other UK ports.

The large-scale clearances of the bomb-damaged city which followed the Second World War resulted in large parts of Hull being rebuilt during the 1950s. The city centre has undergone large-scale changes and modernisation, and its docks have been redeveloped and no longer cater for any mercantile trade. The former Queen's Dock was filled in during the 1930s and the area is now Queen's Gardens; the Humber Dock and Railway Dock have been converted into a thriving marina; and the Prince's Dock, whilst still containing a large expanse of water, is now one of the principal shopping areas following redevelopment during the 1980s and early 1990s.

The people of Hull are proud of their city and their history: they are the descendants of the citizens who defied Charles I, of men who fished some of the most dangerous waters in the world, and of seamen who sailed the perilous Murmansk Run, the Allied lifeline to Russia during the Second World War. One of the most colourful events in Hull's calendar is the annual Marritime Weekend, formerly known as the Sea Fever festival, when Hull's maritime heritage is celebrated.

The story of Hull is full of fascinating characters and events, of which this book can only provide a brief glimpse.

**THE TECHNICAL COLLEGE c1965** H133110

# LOCAL WORDS AND PHRASES

**'A penny all off'** - a short back and sides, as in a hair cut.

**'Bains'** - children.

**'Balling'** - crying.

**'Bray'** - to hit, beat or break.

**'Booling'** - pushing a pram or bike.

**'Flag edge'** - the kerb of the pavement.

**'Gassunder'** - a chamberpot; the term comes from the fact that it 'goes under' the bed.

**'Goin' on rerd'** - going shopping.

**'Larkin'** - playing, messing about.

**'I'm mafted'** - I'm very hot, also **'mafting',** as in **'It's mafting'** - The weather's really hot.

**'Spanish'** - liquorice.

**'Worrawolly'** - a simpleton, fool.

**'Dowly'** - miserable, damp or dreary weather.

**'Nesh'** - cold, as in cold weather.

**'I'm neshed'** - I'm feeling really cold.

**'Taffled'** - tangled.

**'Kecks'** - trousers.

**'Laid out like a shilling dinner'** - Sprawled, as in all over the sofa.

# HAUNTED HULL

Ye Olde White Harte Inn, in an alleyway off Silver Street, has been the location of several mysterious occurrences. Visitors have reported feeling a strange sensation of being watched, particularly in the Functions Room on the second floor, where some customers have complained of being touched, kissed or hit by something invisible, and glasses and bottles have been seen moving across the table, pushed by an unseen hand. There have also been sightings of glowing orbs, and a strange, shimmering shape in the gents' toilet. A skeleton of a woman, apparently murdered, was found in one of the walls of the pub building and her skull, affectionately known as Freda, is kept behind the bar.

> Another of Hull's haunted pubs is the Black Boy on High Street, where bottles of malt whisky are said to 'jump' off shelves, and phantom hands are supposed to materialise from the panelled walls of the hostelry.

Hull's Prospect Centre is built on the site of Hull Royal Infirmary, which was itself built on an area that was used in former times as the site of public executions. The Prospect Centre is linked with many strange stories, and is believed to be haunted by the ghosts of both staff and patients of the Infirmary. Cleaners and staff who work at the centre after the shops have closed often feel uneasy, and some have reported seeing unexplained shadowy figures; other mysterious phenomena include the sound of children's voices, the lift indicator moving even though there is no operator present, items being moved about in stockrooms with no explanation, and rubbish from waste bins being found thrown around the room. One store manager reported seeing a hook on a display board spinning around wildly, and on the occasion of one store's grand opening, a mysterious unidentified extra person was found on the commemorative photograph that was taken.

# HULL MISCELLANY

The statue of William III is shown in photograph H133006, opposite, in the centre of the Market Place. The statue is by the Flemish sculptor Peter Scheemakers, based on the famous equestrian statue of Marcus Aurelius in Rome, and is known locally as 'King Billy'. It was erected by public subscription in 1734 for £893 10s, on the site of Hull's former bullring; it has stood undisturbed for over 250 years, except when it was removed temporarily for safety during the Second World War.

Hull began its life in the 12th century as a hamlet named Wyke upon Hull, which was then in the possession of the monks of nearby Meaux Abbey who had developed a small port for their wool trade. The small town was recognised by Edward I as an ideal location for a supply base for his campaign against the Scots, and was acquired by him in 1293 and subsequently re-named Kingstown (later Kingston) upon Hull. Enjoying royal patronage, it received its first charter in 1299, and after this it soon became one of the foremost ports of the realm, being only surpassed in trade by Liverpool and London.

Kingston upon Hull was fortified during the 14th century when massive brick walls with many towers were constructed to protect the inhabitants; five principal gates gave entry and exit across the moat to the city. Its military importance was recognised again when the city was further fortified during the 16th century. Henry VIII ordered a huge castle to be constructed, but this time on the east bank of the River Hull. The castle, or 'The Citadel' as it was known, was built to a high specification with many bastions, blockhouses and turrets. Sadly, none of the city walls or castle fortifications remain to their original height for the visitor to see, as they were removed for the expansion of the city during the 18th and 19th centuries.

**THE KING WILLIAM STATUE**
**c1955** H133006

THIS STATUE
was Erected in the Year
MDCCXXXIV
To the Memory of
KING WILLIAM The Third
OUR GREAT DELIVERER

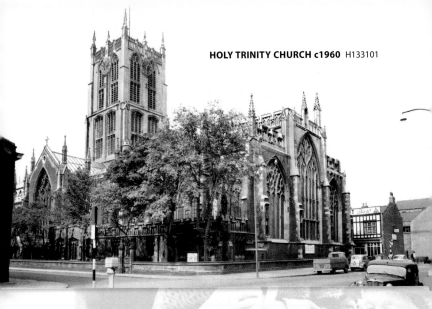

The Church of the Holy and Undivided Trinity, more usually known as Holy Trinity Church (see photograph H133101, above), was originally constructed as a chapel of ease; it did not become a parish church in its own right until 1661, and is reputedly the largest parish church, by area, in the country. The transepts and lower stages of the crossing contain some of the largest and earliest use of medieval brickwork in England. Major restoration work of Holy Trinity Church was carried out internally between 1841 and 1845 under the supervision of the architect Henry Francis Lockwood. The nave was cleared of its galleries, and new pews to the designs of George Peck were fitted, along with a new pulpit of magnesian limestone. The exterior was remodelled between 1859-72 by Sir George Gilbert Scott, and again in 1906 by F S Brodick. The interior of the church is remarkably light and airy, and is lit by some fine windows containing fragments of 15th and 16th century glass. There is a large painting of the Last Supper by James Parmentier (1711), and the aisles and south choir contain examples of medieval tombs, including those of the De La Pole family.

Hull was regarded as a strategic prize by both the Royalists and the Parliamentarians during the Civil War. Local historians will tell you that the war was started in Hull when, on 23 April 1642, Charles I was refused entry to the city; this was the first action of defiance against the king of the Civil War, and set in motion the chain of events that was eventually to lead to his execution. It was in a room now known as the 'Plotting Parlour' in Ye Olde White Harte Inn (then the Governor's home) that the Governor and other leading citizens decided to follow Parliament's instructions and refuse to let Charles I enter Hull and take control of the arsenal that was stored in the city.

Photograph 49814, below, of George Street in 1903 shows the statue of the great poet and patriot Andrew Marvell in its original position. Andrew Marvell was born in March 1621 in the nearby village of Winestead. He was MP for Hull for 20 years, and was a friend of John Milton and an admirer of Oliver Cromwell. The statue of Marvell has moved around Hull to several locations, but now stands in front of Holy Trinity Church.

**GEORGE STREET 1903** 49814

**THE GUILDHALL c1955** H133014

A section of the city walls was excavated a few years ago, and the massive brick foundations were found to be in a wonderful state of preservation. The walls have been preserved in situ, and a viewing area has been constructed around them at the west end of the Whitefriargate.

The west end of Whitefriargate was the site of the Beverley Gate; it was here that Charles I was refused entry in 1642. In later centuries a ceremonial gate or arch was often reconstructed at the west end of the street when subsequent monarchs or members of the royal family visited Hull, perhaps as a token of penance for the citizens having refused the king entry all those years ago.

The church plate of Holy Trinity Church includes a cup, dated 1587, which is the earliest example of a piece of silver bearing the Hull assay mark.

**HOLY TRINITY CHURCH 1903** 49826

**WILBERFORCE HOUSE 1903** 49835

Photograph 49835, above, shows Wilberforce House; according to tradition the house was built and owned during the 16th century by the Lister family, who entertained Charles I here in 1639. The house was extensively added to and remodelled over the years, and contains many architectural features from the 16th to the 20th century. It was here in 1759 that the great emancipator William Wilberforce was born. The Wilberforce family were merchants and corn dealers, and had their own staithe (landing stage) adjoining the house. The house was purchased by the city council in the early 1900s, and was refurbished. It was opened to the public in 1906 as the Wilberforce House Museum, and is now the home of an extensive collection of artefacts relating to the slave trade, the abolition of which was to become the focus of most of William Wilberforce's political life (see page 37).

The first quarter of the 19th century saw Hull become the biggest whaling port in Britain, processing whale oil, seal skins, whale-bone and other attendant products. As the whale fishery came to an end during the 1860s, the city moved forward and became the world's largest centre for oil seed crushing and milling; this led to the establishment of many industries such as paint, colour, oil and varnish manufacture.

Hull's Market Place was for centuries the main area for the city's retail business. It was lined on both sides by every conceivable type of trade or calling, including many taverns and inns with names such as the Reindeer, the Fleece Inn and the Blue Bell. The predominately 19th-century frontages of the Market Place hide the much older buildings contained within, a fact only discovered when large-scale demolition took place along the east side during the 1970s.

**MARKET PLACE 1903** 49813

## Did You Know?
# HULL
### A MISCELLANY

Following the demolition of the northern city walls and the construction of the first dock in 1778, Hull could now spread north and west. The spoil from the excavations was deposited on the Dock Estate Company's land, which slightly raised the surrounding area. George Street was developed by the Hull Dock Company, and was the city's first Georgian suburb. Although Hull lies below sea level, the raising of this area allowed for some grand buildings to be erected, many with sub-basements and cellars. Although once containing some fine residential property, George Street soon became taken over by the business community.

Hull's Guildhall originally occupied a site at the south end of the Market Place not far from Holy Trinity Church, but it had fallen into dereliction by the early 1800s. The Corporation used various buildings as a temporary Guildhall for a number of years, and the foundation stone for a new Guildhall was laid in 1862 on a site to the north of the Market Place, fronting Lowgate between Leadenhall Square and Hanover Square. Four years later the building was completed and is shown in photograph 49805, opposite. It was designed by Cuthbert Broderick in the Italianate or Classical style, and was sumptuously decorated both internally and externally. This Guildhall survived until 1912, when it was demolished, having outgrown its use. Large sections of the building and parts of the tower found a new home in Brantingham, a village to the west of Hull, where a war memorial was constructed from fragments of the fabric, and remaining parts of the tower were placed in Hull's Pearson Park as architectural features. A new Guildhall, to Renaissance designs by Russell, Cooper and Davis, was erected in stages on the same site as the earlier hall between 1903 and 1916, and is shown in photograph H133014 on page 10.

Less than 100 years after the construction of the first dock, the trade of the port was such that Hull required its third major upgrade of its dock offices, resulting in the magnificent Grade II listed building in the Venetian Renaissance style seen in photograph 49806, above. This was designed by Christopher G Wray and built between 1867 and 1871. The triangular-shaped building with its distinctive three domes was acquired by the city council in 1968 and was converted into the Town Docks Museum, which illustrates the importance of fishing, whaling and shipping in Hull's maritime history.

During the late 19th and early 20th centuries, the port of Hull was home to the merchant ships of the Wilson Line; at the beginning of the 20th century this was the world's largest privately-owned mercantile fleet, owning just short of 100 steamships.

The Market Place area of Hull suffered heavily in the Zeppelin air raids of 1915 during the First World War. The Edwin Davis & Co store, on the corner of South Church Side (seen in the centre of photograph 49813 on page 13) was completely obliterated after sustaining a direct hit. The store had occupied the site since 1790, and was probably the only shop in the country to be bombed in both World Wars of the 20th century when its new premises to the north of the city centre suffered the same fate in 1941.

When the traveller and writer Daniel Defoe visited Hull in the 1720s he described it thus: 'The town is exceedingly close built, and should a fire ever be its fate, it might suffer deeply on that account'. The people of Hull were well aware of the fire risk, and firemen's ladders were kept in a prominent position well into the 20th century - one can be seen in photograph 49809, below, on the building just to the right of the church in the centre of the view.

**MARKET PLACE 1903** 49809

In its heyday the River Hull, with its dozens of warehouses and wharves, made a busy highway for the hundreds of large and small craft that earned their living serving the many businesses that lined both banks, and its entrance alongside the Victoria Pier made the pier a popular viewing area. The Humber keel boats, with

their distinctive ketch-rigged sails, and the many paddle steamers were a common sight from the pier. The paddle steamers, such as the 'Isle of Axholme' and the 'Manchester' (seen in the centre of photograph 49821, below) did good business at weekends during the summer months, offering short cruises along the river.

**THE PIER 1903** 49821

**KING EDWARD STREET 1903** 49810

**THE NEW POLICE STATION 1903** 49833

The demolition of large areas of slum property outside the former city walls at the turn of the 20th century created wide thoroughfares and open squares ripe for development. One such area was King Edward Street, which was cleared during the early 1900s to become the focal point for a new city centre and city square. It was surrounded by fine buildings such as the magnificent Prudential Insurance building with its circular tower, designed by Alfred Waterhouse & Son, which can be seen in photograph 49810, opposite. The opening out of the part of the city outside the former city walls also enabled the new electric tram system to operate into the heart of the city and business district. The new square near King Edward Street became a junction for all the city routes. Sadly, this area of the city centre was totally obliterated during the night of 7 May 1941 when it sustained massive damage during the wartime air raids. King Edward Street was completely destroyed, along with Waterworks Street, and fifteen people who were sheltering in the basement of the Prudential Tower tragically lost their lives. The site of the blitzed Prudential Insurance building became the new Queen's House development in 1951.

Photograph 49833, opposite, shows the newly-built police headquarters on Alfred Gelder Street, which opened on 25 March 1904. The new building replaced the old central police station which had occupied the site of the former Charity Hall around the corner in nearby Parliament Street. The new building contained 24 cells, and was built in a 'U' shape with offices flanking the corridors. It closed in the 1950s and the site was sold to the Littlewoods group for an extension to their department store.

Paragon Street took its name from the late 18th-century inn of the same name which occupied the corner of the nearby Chariot Street. The street was laid out c1802, and soon many taverns, hotels, inns and shops were built, including the White Horse Hotel (seen in photograph 49815, opposite), an oasis of temperance amongst its neighbours. The building was a tea and coffee house belonging to the Hull People's Public House Company, and was one of eighteen in the city which provided a decent lunch and a non-alcoholic drink for the working man. Being surrounded on all sides by the alcoholic attractions of its neighbours, the White Horse was eventually forced to concede defeat and became licensed during the 1920s; it is now the large and imposing Yates Wine Lodge.

Waterworks Street was an old street that took its name from its close proximity to Hull's first waterworks, which were situated in this area in the 17th century. Following its destruction in the Second World War it became the eastern extension of Paragon Street, when the destroyed and badly damaged 19th-century buildings were swept away to build a unified city centre. Although extensively redeveloped, Paragon Street retains several of its older buildings, and also a magnificent late 19th-century Grade II listed Gothic Revival roofed arcade, designed by Sir Alfred Gelder.

HMS 'Bounty', famous for the mutiny of its crew on the island of Tahiti, was built at Hull in 1784. The vessel was originally a merchant ship called the 'Bethia', and was purchased by the Admiralty in 1787 and renamed.

**PARAGON STREET 1903** 49815

**PARAGON STREET c1960** H133068

**THE PIER 1903** 49823

In 1868 the old 50-gun HMS 'Southampton' arrived on the river, where she became a sail training ship and boys' reformatory. She can be seen centre left of photograph 49823, above, and remained part of the waterfront scene for over 40 years.

The Humber Iron Works can be seen on the extreme left of photograph 49823, above. These works, on the east bank of the River Hull entrance, occupied the site of Martin Samuelson's shipyard, which in 1863 had built more iron-clad ships than any other yard in the kingdom. So famous was the yard that to this day the site is still known as 'Sammy's Point'. It is now the home of Hull's millennium project, a marine life centre entitled 'The Deep'.

Ferries had existed over the River Humber, a natural barrier between Yorkshire and Lincolnshire, since the 14th century; Barton, Barrow, Goxhill and New Holland all had their own ferries connecting with the city. The ferry boat dock had originally occupied a site inside the entrance to the River Hull, but trade increased to such an extent that by the beginning of the 19th century a purpose-built ferry boat dock was constructed on land reclaimed from the River Humber and part of the old Artillery Ground at the south end. A dock in name only, it took the form of a wooden pier constructed parallel with the River Humber to facilitate landings in rough seas - see photograph 49820, below.

**THE HUMBER 1903** 49820

25

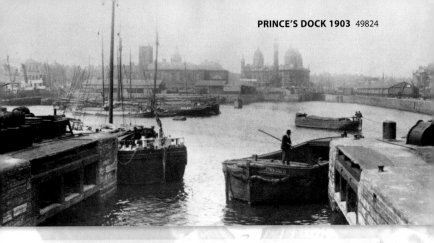

Hull's success as a port meant that its facilities were continually upgraded to keep up with trade following the construction of the first dock in 1778. Three more docks were to follow: Humber Dock in 1809, Junction Dock (later Prince's Dock) in 1829, and the Railway Dock in 1846. When Junction Dock opened, it formed the last link of a chain of three docks that connected the River Hull with the River Humber, encircling the Old Town along the line of the former fortifications. The dock was renamed Prince's Dock in 1854 following a visit by Queen Victoria and Prince Albert, the Prince Consort.

Photograph 49824, above, shows Prince's Dock in 1903. This dock served, amongst others, the UK ports of Aberdeen, Ipswich and Grangemouth, along with the continental ports of Rotterdam, Hamburg and Bremen. As ships became larger, Prince's Dock's trade declined as larger docks were built to the east and west of the city. Its trade relied on the smaller coastal craft and the city's trawler fleet, whose ships were fitted out in the nearby yard of C D Holmes Engineering Co. Following its closure in 1968, Prince's Dock remained derelict for a number of years. However, it still survives following its redevelopment as the Prince's Quay shopping centre, which is built on stilts; the dock retains a large expanse of water and its original walls.

From the mid 19th century onwards Hull expanded in all directions, and more docks were needed to keep pace with the boom in trade. Outside the confinements of the Old Town, a new dock, Victoria Dock, was planned to run parallel to the River Humber, and this time it was to be on the east shore of the River Hull. The Victoria Dock was opened in 1850, in an area once occupied by the ancient hamlet of Drypool, and rapidly became the home of Hull's timber import trade from the Scandinavian and Baltic ports. A booming export trade in coal meant that the newly-emptied coal wagons could immediately fill with pit props from the timber yards for their return journey to the West Riding coalfields of Yorkshire. There was also a large foreign cattle depot with slaughterhouses and chilling facilities, which was constructed to handle the importation of animals from the Americas. The Victoria Dock closed in 1970 and the area is now a rapidly expanding 'dockland village', with hundreds of waterside houses alongside the River Humber.

**WEST PARK 1903** 49836

**ALBERT DOCK c1955** H133041

**ST ANDREW'S DOCK c1955** H133037

Following the discovery of the Silver Pits fishing grounds in the North Sea in 1850, Hull's fishing industry saw a sudden and massive expansion take place. Dock space for both fishing and mercantile interests was now at a premium, and a new dock was opened in 1869. This was known throughout its construction as the Western Dock, but on the day of its opening it was named the Albert Dock, after Albert Edward, Prince of Wales (later Edward VII), who performed the ceremony. Initially the home of the fishing fleet, the Albert Dock soon became the dock for the importation of wood pulp, paper, fruit and provisions and for the export of heavy vehicles, cars and industrial and agricultural machinery. The dock is still open today, but with the reduction in cargo handling due to containerisation the Albert Dock has once again become the home of the city's fishing fleet.

St Andrew's Dock (see photograph H133037, opposite) was originally intended for the use of the coal industry, but immediately after opening in 1883 it was named after the patron saint of fishermen and handed over for the exclusive use of Hull's 420 fishing smacks. The fishing industry expanded and became so successful that by 1895 an extension was commissioned, which opened in 1897. By the early years of the 20th century St Andrew's Dock had become home to the world's largest deep-water fishing fleet. St Andrew's Dock was unique in that all the main activities concerned with the upkeep and maintenance of a large fishing fleet took place on and around the dock estate. The dock had the largest ice manufactory in Europe, capable of producing over 1,000 tons a day; the largest fishmeal plant in the world; the busiest postal and telegraph office in the country; and several banks, shops and cafes. An economic survey of the 1950s stated that there were probably around 50,000 people in Hull, or one fifth of the population, involved with the fishing industry. Sadly, St Andrew's Dock closed in 1975, and the site has now been redeveloped as the St Andrew's Quay leisure and retail complex; hardly any trace remains now of Hull's once great fishing tradition.

From the 1770s the Hull Dock Company had enjoyed carte blanche regarding shipping facilities in the port, but this was to change during the 1880s with the formation of the Hull, Barnsley & West Riding Junction Railway & Dock Company. A new dock was begun in 1881 on a site to the east of the Victoria Dock; it was almost twice the size of anything built so far. On opening in 1885 it was named after Princess Alexandra, the wife of the Prince of Wales. The dock was the first to be built in Hull for the accommodation of the much larger and newer steam vessels then rapidly taking over from sail. As trade increased to all parts of the world the dock soon became home to all manner of goods and commodities, including large quantities of timber, fruit and vegetables, and grain and oil seeds of every description. Ships with exotic home ports such as Vera Cruz, Rosario, Pernambuco, Karachi and Havana were a common sight in the dock following the establishment of the long trade routes to Australia, South America and Asia. The dock closed in 1982, but owing to the increased demand for port facilities it re-opened to shipping in 1991.

The last piece in the jigsaw of Hull's docks arrived just before the First World War, with the opening of the first dock in the country to use electric power throughout. Built jointly by the Hull & Barnsley Railway Company and the North Eastern Railway Company, it was originally to be called the Joint Dock, but it was renamed King George Dock on its opening on 26 June 1914 by George V. This was the largest of Hull's nine docks, with a total water area of 53 acres. The massive coal exports that left the port and the huge amount of grain that came into the country through this dock were to dominate its trade for many years. With its 23 coaling berths, its 40,000-ton grain silo, its three acres of wool sheds and its tea, fruit, meat and vegetable transit sheds, the dock was a hive of activity. The dock still thrives today, and is the English home of the P&O North Sea Ferries Company, who use the largest roll-on roll-off ferries in the world to serve the European ports of Rotterdam and Zeebrugge.

**ALEXANDRA DOCK c1955** H133048

**KING GEORGE DOCK c1960** H133058

**EAST PARK, THE BOATING LAKE c1965**  H133103

Until the 18th century, all shipping arriving in Hull unloaded its wares at private staithes, or landing stages, adjoining the warehouses on the west bank of the Old Harbour of the River Hull. The huge trade of the port was causing concern to the Customs and Excise, who had no provision for a legal quay where goods could be appraised. The Dock Act of 1774 was to change all this, with the creation of the Hull Dock Company, the first statutory dock company in Britain. In 1778 a new dock of 10 acres, then the largest inland dock in the country, was opened at right angles to, and entered from, the River Hull. Originally known as the Dock until the creation of the Humber Dock in 1809, it subsequently became the Old Dock. It was finally called Queen's Dock following a visit by Queen Victoria in 1854 when she sailed through the whole line of docks from the River Hull to the River Humber. The dock closed in 1930, and following reclamation the site was redeveloped as the municipal Queen's Gardens.

The Hull Savings Bank was established in 1818. It occupied various sites throughout the city before becoming established in Posterngate, where it remained for over 50 years. The expansion and growth of banking reflected Hull's rise as a trading centre, and the Hull Savings Bank moved to new premises at the junction of George Street and Smeaton Street in 1884 (see photograph 49814 on page 9), built to the designs of Robert Clamp. The bank was unusual in that it had its own elementary school between 1831-51, the only known example anywhere in the country.

**THE DOCK OFFICES 1903** 49807

**ALEXANDRA DOCK c1955** H133045

**UNLOADING AT VICTORIA DOCK c1955** H133044

The corner opposite the Hull Savings Bank in photograph 49814 on page 9 (right of photograph) was redeveloped around 1884 as a retail wine and spirit vaults belonging to Henry Wilson, a wine and spirit merchant; the vaults adjoined his large offices, which were known as Savile House. The public house, built in gin palace style, and the grand offices were known thereafter as Wilson's Corner. Although the offices have disappeared, the public house remains unaltered and is still known by many people locally as Wilson's Corner, although its official name is the Dram Shop.

Hull was one of the few towns or cities in Britain that suffered badly during both World Wars of the 20th century, as it was bombed during both conflicts. During the Second World War Hull was the most bombed centre of occupation after London, sustaining 82 air raids with 1,200 people killed and over 3,000 injured. Out of a housing stock of 92,660, only 5,945 houses remained unscathed, and most of the grand buildings which once adorned the main thoroughfares of Hull were either obliterated or seriously damaged.

When the Humber Bridge was opened in 1981 it was the largest single-span suspension bridge in the world, at 4,626ft long. The total length of wire in the cables of the bridge is 44,000 miles - more than 1½ times the circumference of the Earth.

**THE DOCK OFFICES AND THE WILBERFORCE MONUMENT 1903** 49808

The Doric column seen in the centre of photograph 49808, above, is a monument to William Wilberforce - the first stone was laid on 1 August 1834, the date on which slavery in the British Empire became illegal. The tall fluted column is 90ft high, and is surmounted by a 12ft statue, and cost £1,250, funded by public subscription. The Wilberforce Memorial is seen in this photograph in its original position, close to the Dock Offices and near to the bridge over the lock gates connecting Prince's Dock and Queen's Dock - the bridge was henceforth known as Monument Bridge, and although both the lock gates and the bridge carrying the road have long since disappeared, this area is still known as Monument Bridge. Owing to traffic problems encountered following large-scale improvements to the area, the Wilberforce Monument was moved to a site at the east end of Queen's Gardens in 1935.

William Wilberforce was born in Hull in 1759, and was elected MP for Hull at the age of 21. He was involved in many causes for reform during his lifetime, but is best remembered for his long campaign against slavery which resulted in the passing of a parliamentary bill to end the slave trade in 1807, and slavery being abolished in the British Empire in 1833 (this became law in 1834). Wilberforce died in 1833, and was buried in Westminster Abbey. He was named the Greatest Ever Yorkshireman in a BBC poll in 2000, and in June 2005 Archbishop Desmond Tutu praised him, saying that 'Wilberforce showed that each and every one of us can make a difference'.

Much of the property in Hull's Old Town and Market Place evolved over several hundred years; it was a mixture of large riverside warehouses, commercial properties, small businesses and scattered areas of housing. Hull's situation on the east side of the country meant that most of its trade was conducted with the Scandinavian countries, the Baltic States, the Hanseatic ports and the low countries of Europe. The centre of Hull's merchant trade was conducted in the High Street alongside the 'Old Harbour' (the name given to the lower reaches of the River Hull where it entered the River Humber). The High Street, formerly known as Hull Street, followed the line of the river; the merchants built many substantial and richly-adorned houses along its frontage adjoining their staithes, or private wharves. The names of the merchants who built these houses or were associated with them are reflected in the superb examples that survive today: Blaydes House, the Maister House, Crowle House and Wilberforce House.

Several Hull merchants became very wealthy and influential. One family in particular, the De La Poles, progressed from their beginnings as humble merchants to become aldermen and mayors of the city; they eventually rose to be the richest merchant family in the land, and were created Earls of Suffolk under Richard II. The family built a huge mansion named the Suffolk Palace opposite St Mary's Church, Lowgate, on a site later occupied by Hull's General Post Office, now a large public house belonging to the J D Wetherspoon chain.

The Cross Keys Hotel can be seen in photograph 49809 on page 17. The building stood on the east side of the Market Place, and took its name from the Archbishops of York, who had a hostelry in this area during the 14th century; their coat of arms consisted of two crossed keys, the sign of St Peter. The building had been an important coaching inn since the 18th century and had 40 bedrooms and 15 sitting rooms, some of which were named after great national heroes, such as the Wellington Room, the Nelson Room and the Raleigh Room. Trade at the hotel declined in the late 19th century, and the Cross Keys closed in 1922; by 1937 the building had become almost derelict. Just prior to its demolition it was described in the local paper, the Hull Daily Mail, as being 'a large and impressive four-storied building with a double front and stabling for 40 horses. To the rear is a great courtyard in which hangs a bell dated 1596, along with great branches of decorated ironwork from which the oil lamps swung when the steaming horses clattered in a winter's night'.

**HYMERS COLLEGE 1903** 49834

**ST MATTHEW'S CHURCH, ANLABY ROAD 1903** 49832

Whitefriargate, and its eastern extensions of Silver Street and Scale Lane, is part of an ancient street named Aldgate leading from the Beverley Gate deep into the heart of the Old Town. The name Whitefriargate is derived from the road's position alongside the site of a friary belonging to the Carmelites, or White Friars. There was once also a Blackfriargate, which was named after the Dominicans who had a religious foundation near to the Market Place. Whitefriargate was always a popular business area lined with many fine shops, banks, hotels and taverns. Large-scale redevelopment has taken place in the area, especially along the north side of the street. Whitefriargate is now fully pedestrianised, but the street retains many of its late 18th- and early 19th-century buldings, and above the modern shop fronts the original fine architectural building lines show the modern visitor a glimpse of the street's former grandeur.

The famous New Amphitheatre was built in 1846 at the junction of Paragon Street with South Street: with its Paragon Street frontage of 206ft in length, and seating approximately 3,000 people, it was at one time one of the largest theatres in the country. Following many name changes, the building was partially demolished after becoming unsafe. In 1871 the grand Italianate structure known as the Imperial Hotel was built on the site of its auditorium; remodelled and rebuilt, the theatre opened as a smaller venue named the Theatre Royal which itself closed in 1909, and the building was reopened as the Tivoli Theatre in 1912. Arthur Lucan, of 'Old Mother Riley' fame, tragically died in the theatre on 17 May 1954 just before going on stage for a performance of 'Old Mother Riley in Paris', and is buried in Hull's Eastern Cemetery.

# SPORTING HULL

**Hull City Football Club** was formed in 1903 and was originally based at a site on the north side of Anlaby Road near St Matthew's Church. The club moved to a new ground on Boothferry Road in 1947, and has now moved to a brand new state of the art stadium near to its original site on Anlaby Road, which is shared with **Hull FC** (Rugby League). A record attendance at a Division Three game was set at Boothferry Park on Christmas Day 1948, when 49,655 people attended a game against Rotherham.

Hull City Football Club player **David Mercer** played every single game played by the club during the First World War, part of a run of 218 consecutive appearances for the Tigers.

When **Hull Kingston Rovers** moved to the New Craven Park for the 1989/90 season, the main stand had a unique feature: it was built with 8 hospitality boxes, and was the first Rugby League ground in England to feature such a facility.

**Hull FC** has the rather dubious distinction of having lost more major finals than any other club, including three successive challenge Cup Finals between 1908 and 1920. Here are two rather better records:

- In the 1978/79 season in Division Two, **Hull FC** won every game. This is the only time this has been achieved in professional Rugby League.

- **Hull FC's Lee Jackson** holds the record for the fastest ever try in a professional game. Playing against Sheffield Eagles at the Don Valley Stadium in 1992, he scored after just nine seconds.

# QUIZ QUESTIONS

Answers on page 48.

1. Which fictional traveller embarked from the port of Hull on the sea voyage which resulted in him being castaway on a desert island?

2. Which architect has been described by some historians as doing for Hull what Sir Christopher Wren had done for London?

3. What is the origin of the name of Carr Lane?

4. Which famous novelist and poet was chief librarian of the Brynmor Jones Library at Hull University from 1955 until his death in 1985?

5. Which is the only surviving Victorian church in Hull with a spire?

6. What is the fanciful local story linked with the statue of William III on his horse in the Market Place?

7. On the corner of Boulevard and Hessel Road stands the Fishermen's Memorial, a statue of George Smith, skipper of the Hull trawler 'Crane'. Smith was killed during an incident known as 'The Russian Outrage' - what was this?

8. The Town Docks Museum holds examples of scrimshaw carvings - what are these?

9. Who holds the title of 'Admiral of the Humber'?

10. Which famous name in aviation history was born in Hull in 1903?

**THE QUEEN VICTORIA STATUE**
**c1955** H133011

43

**QUEEN'S GARDENS c1955** H133026

# RECIPE

## COD, LEMON AND LIME FISHCAKES
*This recipe is a reminder of Hull's deep-water fishing tradition.*

**Ingredients**

750g/1½lb thick cod fillet

450g/1lb large new potatoes, scrubbed and parboiled

Half an onion, grated

Zest of 1 lemon and 1 lime

Juice of 1 lime

Salt and freshly ground black pepper

2 tablespoonfuls sunflower oil

Place the cod fillet in a pan, and cover with water. Heat until the water simmers for 2 minutes, then turn off the heat, cover the pan and leave to cool. Alternatively the fish can be cooked in a microwave, covered with film, on a high setting for about 3 minutes, and then left to cool. When cooked and cooled, flake the fish into large pieces.

Grate the potatoes into a bowl, and add the flaked fish and grated onion, the lemon and lime zest and lime juice. Season with salt and freshly ground black pepper to taste. Shape the mix with your hands on a floured surface into 8 thick fishcakes, place them on a plate and leave to rest in the fridge for 10 minutes.

Heat the oil in a frying pan and fry the fish cakes on one side until they are crusty and browned, then turn them and cook the other sides.

# RECIPE

## YORKSHIRE FAT RASCALS

These delicious fruited teacakes with a rich crust are a sort of cross between scones and rock cakes, and are a favourite delicacy in many a Yorkshire tearoom. The original versions would have been cooked in Yorkshire homes either on a 'backstone' or on a griddle over a turf fire, and they were also known as turf cakes in the past. The use of glacé cherries and candied peel is a more recent addition. This quantity should make 8 Fat Rascals.

### Ingredients

225g/8oz self-raising flour

115g/4oz butter or margarine, cut into small pieces

75g/3oz caster sugar or light soft brown sugar

Pinch of salt

50g/2oz mixed dried fruit – currants, raisins, sultanas

25g/1oz glacé cherries, cut in half

25g/1oz chopped candied mixed peel

1 egg

3-4 tablespoonfuls of milk

Pre-heat the oven to 200°C/400°F/Gas Mark 6, grease 2 baking sheets and line them with baking parchment or greaseproof paper.

Sift the flour into a mixing bowl, add the cubed fat and use your fingertips to rub it into the flour until the mixture resembles fine breadcrumbs (or prepare in a food processor if preferred). Add the sugar, salt, lemon and orange zest, dried fruit, cherries and peel, and mix well. Beat the egg and stir it into the mixture, adding just enough milk to form the mixture into a firm ball of dough – it should not be too wet and sticky.

Lightly flour your hands, and divide the dough into 8 pieces, rolling each piece very lightly between your hands to form it into a ball. Arrange the balls of dough on the prepared baking sheets, dust them with a little caster sugar and bake in the pre-heated oven for about 15-20 minutes, until they are risen and golden brown but before the dried fruit starts to burn. They can be eaten warm from the oven or cold, either just as they are or spread with butter.

# QUIZ ANSWERS

1.  Robinson Crusoe, in the novel by Daniel Defoe.

2.  Sir William Alfred Gelder (1855-1943), who was the son of a West Hull village farmer, a self-made man and a successful architect. He was Lord Mayor of Hull in five successive years, MP for Brigg, and was knighted in 1903. His plans, around the turn of the 20th century, for clearing the city centre of dilapidated slum property by creating wide and airy thoroughfares was to shape Hull into the layout which still exists today. The early 1900s saw a new street constructed through a very unsavoury district to link the bridge spanning the River Hull at Drypool. It was named Alfred Gelder Street in honour of the man who had done so much to re-form and re-shape Hull.

3.  Carr is a corruption of the Norse word 'kjarr', meaning 'wet, boggy marshlands'. The area immediately to the west of Hull was indeed always wet, marshy and prone to flooding.

4.  Philip Larkin. In his poem 'Here', he describes Hull thus:

    'Here domes and statues, spires and cranes cluster
    Beside grain-scattered streets, barge-crowded water …'

5.  The only surviving Victorian church in Hull with a spire is St Matthew's Church in Anlaby Road (see photograph 49832, on page 39). The church was erected in 1870 at a cost of £7,000 to the designs of Adams & Kelly. It remains a prominent landmark for the surrounding area, and is described by Pevsner as the most impressive Victorian church in this part of the city.

6.  Local lore says that when the king hears the clock of the nearby Holy Trinity Church strike midnight, he dismounts and avails himself of a drink in the nearby King William Hotel.

7. 'The Russian Outrage' was an incident which occurred in 1904. Russia was at war with Japan, and in the early hours of 22 October 1904 the Russian fleet opened fire on a group of Hull trawlers fishing on the Dogger Bank, mistaking them for Japanese torpedo boats. George Smith was killed instantly; his trawler was sunk and three other trawlers were damaged.

8. The scrimshaw carvings in the Town Docks Museum are a reminder of Hull's former importance as a whaling centre, when Hull men sailed the northern waters around Greenland and Spitsbergen in search of whales, at that time a valuable source of oil for use in lamps and as a lubricant. Sailors occupied themselves on these long voyages by carving intricate designs on whale teeth or walrus tusks using the blade of a knife or a sail needle, and then highlighted the design by rubbing lampblack or ink into the incised lines. The carvings became known as scrimshaw, and are now highly prized by collectors.

9. The title of 'Admiral of the Humber' is held by the Lord Mayor of Hull.

10. Hull was the birthplace of the pioneering aviatrix Amy Johnson (1903-1941), who became a national heroine when she became the first female pilot to fly solo from Britain to Australia, at the age of 26, in 1930. She began the historic flight in her de Havilland DH60 Gipsy Moth G-AAAH from Croydon Airport on 5 May 1930. She landed at Port Darwin, on the northern tip of Australia, nineteen days later, after flying 9,960 miles on a dangerous and eventful trip. Amy died during the Second World War, when the plane she was ferrying for the RAF disappeared over the Thames Estuary. She is commemorated in Hull by a statue in Prospect Street.

**ALEXANDRA DOCK 1903** 49825

...TH & SON

...ANS & GAS·FITTERS  46

GAS
FITTINGS

PLUMBING

NATIONAL
594
TELEPHONE

WATCH,
CLOCK
AND
JEWELLERY
REPAIRS

CARR LANE 1903  49816

# FRANCIS FRITH

## PIONEER VICTORIAN PHOTOGRAPHER

Francis Frith, founder of the world-famous photographic archive, was a complex and multi-talented man. A devout Quaker and a highly successful Victorian businessman, he was philosophical by nature and pioneering in outlook. By 1855 he had already established a wholesale grocery business in Liverpool, and sold it for the astonishing sum of £200,000, which is the equivalent today of over £15,000,000. Now in his thirties, and captivated by the new science of photography, Frith set out on a series of pioneering journeys up the Nile and to the Near East.

## INTRIGUE AND EXPLORATION

He was the first photographer to venture beyond the sixth cataract of the Nile. Africa was still the mysterious 'Dark Continent', and Stanley and Livingstone's historic meeting was a decade into the future. The conditions for picture taking confound belief. He laboured for hours in his wicker dark-room in the sweltering heat of the desert, while the volatile chemicals fizzed dangerously in their trays. Back in London he exhibited his photographs and was 'rapturously cheered' by members of the Royal Society. His reputation as a photographer was made overnight.

## VENTURE OF A LIFE-TIME

By the 1870s the railways had threaded their way across the country, and Bank Holidays and half-day Saturdays had been made obligatory by Act of Parliament. All of a sudden the working man and his family were able to enjoy days out, take holidays, and see a little more of the world.

With typical business acumen, Francis Frith foresaw that these new tourists would enjoy having souvenirs to commemorate their days out. For the next thirty years he travelled the country by train and by pony and trap, producing fine photographs of seaside resorts and beauty spots that were keenly bought by millions of Victorians. These prints were painstakingly pasted into family albums and pored over during the dark nights of winter, rekindling precious memories of summer excursions. Frith's studio was soon supplying retail shops all over the country, and by 1890 F Frith & Co had become the greatest specialist photographic publishing company in the world, with over 2,000 sales outlets, and pioneered the picture postcard.

## FRANCIS FRITH'S LEGACY

Francis Frith had died in 1898 at his villa in Cannes, his great project still growing. By 1970 the archive he created contained over a third of a million pictures showing 7,000 British towns and villages.

Frith's legacy to us today is of immense significance and value, for the magnificent archive of evocative photographs he created provides a unique record of change in the cities, towns and villages throughout Britain over a century and more. Frith and his fellow studio photographers revisited locations many times down the years to update their views, compiling for us an enthralling and colourful pageant of British life and character.

We are fortunate that Frith was dedicated to recording the minutiae of everyday life. For it is this sheer wealth of visual data, the painstaking chronicle of changes in dress, transport, street layouts, buildings, housing and landscape that captivates us so much today, offering us a powerful link with the past and with the lives of our ancestors.

Computers have now made it possible for Frith's many thousands of images to be accessed almost instantly. The archive offers every one of us an opportunity to examine the places where we and our families have lived and worked down the years. Its images, depicting our shared past, are now bringing pleasure and enlightenment to millions around the world a century and more after his death.

For further information visit: www.francisfrith.com

## INTERIOR DECORATION

Frith's photographs can be seen framed and as giant wall murals in thousands of pubs, restaurants, hotels, banks, retail stores and other public buildings throughout Britain. These provide interesting and attractive décor, generating strong local interest and acting as a powerful reminder of gentler days in our increasingly busy and frenetic world.

## FRITH PRODUCTS

All Frith photographs are available as prints and posters in a variety of different sizes and styles. In the UK we also offer a range of other gift and stationery products illustrated with Frith photographs, although many of these are not available for delivery outside the UK – see our web site for more information on the products available for delivery in your country.

## THE INTERNET

Over 100,000 photographs of Britain can be viewed and purchased on the Frith web site. The web site also includes memories and reminiscences contributed by our customers, who have personal knowledge of localities and of the people and properties depicted in Frith photographs. If you wish to learn more about a specific town or village you may find these reminiscences fascinating to browse. Why not add your own comments if you think they would be of interest to others? See **www.francisfrith.com**

## PLEASE HELP US BRING FRITH'S PHOTOGRAPHS TO LIFE

Our authors do their best to recount the history of the places they write about. They give insights into how particular towns and villages developed, they describe the architecture of streets and buildings, and they discuss the lives of famous people who lived there. But however knowledgeable our authors are, the story they tell is necessarily incomplete.

Frith's photographs are so much more than plain historical documents. They are living proofs of the flow of human life down the generations. They show real people at real moments in history; and each of those people is the son or daughter of someone, the brother or sister, aunt or uncle, grandfather or grandmother of someone else. All of them lived, worked and played in the streets depicted in Frith's photographs.

We would be grateful if you would give us your insights into the places shown in our photographs: the streets and buildings, the shops, businesses and industries. Post your memories of life in those streets on the Frith website: what it was like growing up there, who ran the local shop and what shopping was like years ago; if your workplace is shown tell us about your working day and what the building is used for now. Read other visitors' memories and reconnect with your shared local history and heritage. With your help more and more Frith photographs can be brought to life, and vital memories preserved for posterity, and for the benefit of historians in the future.

Wherever possible, we will try to include some of your comments in future editions of our books. Moreover, if you spot errors in dates, titles or other facts, please let us know, because our archive records are not always completely accurate—they rely on 140 years of human endeavour and hand-compiled records. You can email us using the contact form on the website.

Thank you!

For further information, trade, or author enquiries
please contact us at the address below:

**The Francis Frith Collection, Oakley Business Park,
Wylye Road, Dinton, Wiltshire SP3 5EU.**
Tel: +44 (0)1722 716 376  Fax: +44 (0)1722 716 881
e-mail: sales@francisfrith.co.uk  **www.francisfrith.com**